Under Watchful Eyes

poems by

Mark Schardine

Under Watchful Eyes

Cover Photo: *"La Loge de l'opéra"* Constantin Guys

ISBN- 978-1-7374758-4-2

Published by:

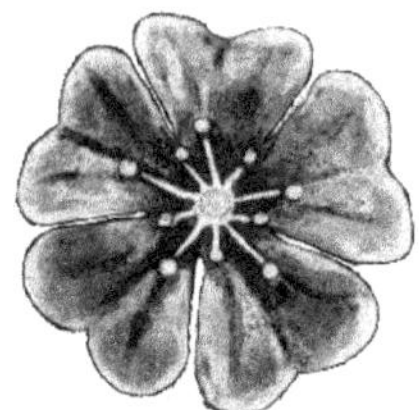

Blue Jade Press, LLC

Blue Jade Press, LLC
Vineland, NJ 08360
www.bluejadepress.com

Acknowledgements

Francis Davis Millet, "The Unconverted" (n.d.). Oil on canvas, 30 1/2 x 50 1/2 in. (77.47 x 128.27 cm.). Gift of Tom and Jean Meade (2017.42) | PAFA Pennsylvania Academy of the Fine Arts

Introduction

A poem should not exist simply as words on a page. It should allow the reader to bring the words to life by reading it aloud, and inspire the reader's imagination to interpret it in multiple ways. We often associate poetry with music, and a reader will find different ways to recite a poem, to allow the sounds to have an impact. Indeed, many actors and actresses refine their vocal skills by reading poetry. The reader will furthermore create images of the poem, visualize the scene presented or the story told. A poem can take on a photographic or cinematic quality, as readers close their eyes and see myriad scenes unfold, and each reading can allow a new creative experience.

Unsurprisingly, the visual arts can easily fascinate poets. A photograph, a painting, a sculpture, or a movie can cause poets to spend hours pondering them, seeking to understand these works and find a new meaning each time. So too must a poem's words trigger a response, one that results from the refinement and wit of the poem, but more importantly, because the ideas expressed do not allow the reader to remain indifferent. They remain to be recalled again and again, as each time the reader finds pleasure and insight, and at times must also recognize that we cannot avoid the sorrows in our lives, but accept the full impact they will have on us.

Table of Contents

The Sea

Mermaids

Romance

Culinary

Widows

The Muse

Errors

Absinthe

Politics

Seeking Meaning

Temptations

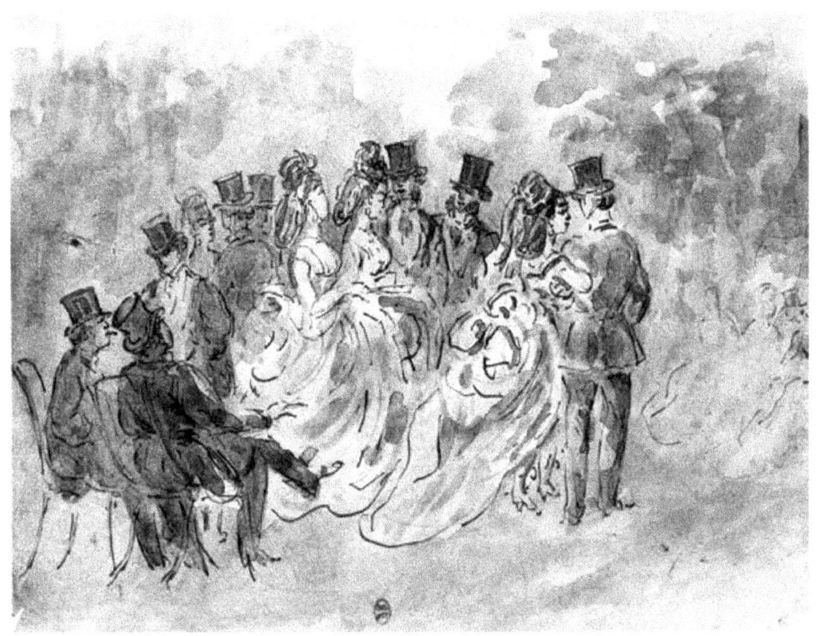

Lurking

Cocktails served poolside
Evening gowns, tuxedos,
Husbands, wives, lovers,
An extra guest has arrived
Well, she invited herself.

People have seen her
Men who recall her swimsuit
Now notice her dress,
She strikes up conversations
No one will ask her to leave.

She blends in quite well
Waiters find a place for her
The first course arrives
Her watchful eyes scan the scene
Nothing will escape her view.

Keeping Paparazzi Employed

On Fifth Avenue
She steps out of her limo
Right on schedule
Long sleek black gem-studded dress
Every angle is seen.

Not Passing Unnoticed

Her dreaming dark eyes
Jet black hair on her shoulders
Magenta swimsuit
Attract our wandering gaze
To a seaside photograph.

A Young Courtesan

In the Grand Hotel
Her silk dress and smooth black gloves
Dark hair's glossy sheen
Calm alluring expression
Win the staff's admiration.

At the best table
She sips a Champagne cocktail
Dreamily looks out
Stares at waves reaching the shore
Maintains a wistful smile.

Packages arrive
The front desk takes care of them
She will soon find them
For these frequent costly gifts
She is, of course, most grateful.

A starry night falls
She thinks of tomorrow's plans
A leisurely stroll
Bikini and sunglasses
Chats with boys who sell ice cream.

As she dines alone
Sees waiters promptly reply
Many husbands sigh
Oh, the money they give her
Maybe one man will please her.

An Elegant Lady

Her spotless white dress
Smooth bejeweled velvet gloves
Modest polite grin
Allow her to win favor
Wanton men make way for her.

Street Side Café Scene

Ready for a chat
Affecting a relaxed air
She expects him soon
Her chance to see his mind change
But what is making him late?

Rewards for the Bold

A clever dandy
Confident, charming, handsome,
Owns not a penny
Uses witty words to flirt
And often enough succeeds.

No One Is Blind

Coming from the pool
Glistening in the summer sun
In her snug swimsuit
Aware of how men see her
Intentions they do not hide.

Nothing Harmful Foreseen

All is in order
The photo shoot can begin
She stands by the pool
Image captured by a lens
For a man who will stalk her.

No Confidence Betrayed

She always helped you
Arranged each secret meeting
Word never got out.

Each time at dinner
You saw her savor Champagne
Show off her silk dress
Suggest what she had in mind
Offer you a wistful grin.

Far from her husband
She freely conversed with you
Left out no details
Let you know what awaited
All the pleasure she would give.

Yes, she adored you
Spared no effort to please you
But there were others.

A Courtesan in Her Forties

She still had her friends
Men who remembered her well
Valued her friendship.

On all her nights' out
A man confided secrets
She was most discreet.

Always a kind word
Levity, humor, joy, fun
He could feel at ease.

She kept her figure
Followed the latest fashions
She could still turn heads.

After a dinner
She sometimes asked him to stay
He always agreed.

She had many friends
They never tired of her
No man disliked her.

With her wit, grace, charm
Doors always opened for her
Red carpets rolled out

Others may have had problems
But that never bothered her.

After the Fashion Show

Her hair disheveled
She slowly takes off her gloves
Tears fall on her dress,
Along with letters from fans
Her divorce papers arrived.

No Legal Misunderstanding

The letter arrived
Grounds for divorce were explained
No doubt could remain
Although it caught him off-guard
She had planned it all along.

Quick Irrevocable Decision

She called her lawyer
The time had come for divorce
He was such a bore.

He asked her to stay
They had spent years together
She would not listen.

People were quite shocked
There seemed no reason for it
Yet she insisted.

We saw her later
Strolling alone in the mall
As if all was well.

She Does Catch Her Thief

Cruising in her boat
She chats most freely with him
Shows him old hideouts.

She asks him to stay
He understands things so well
Why not take the plunge?
What a team the two would make
Very much loot to be had.

As he hesitates
She stares at him and points out
Loot of his she found.

What Must Remain Concealed

You see her smile
How she stares into your eyes
Suggests you kiss her
Offers her velvet sheathed hands
Now at evening's begin.

She removed her ring
Will not speak of her husband
Tonight is for you.

Listen to her words
She has much to say to you
Let her flatter you
Give hints of what awaits you
Persuade you to embrace her.

She seems most happy
Aware how she can keep you
Caught in the scandal.

Sweet Memories

She remembers you
The nights the two of you met
In places she chose
You never kept her waiting
She valued your discretion.

She enjoyed those times
You always did what she asked
It delighted her.

When it had to end
She felt sympathy for you
One last soft caress
Though this affair had pleased her
People had begun to talk.

You Never Mention Her Name

Always most discreet
She never divulged secrets
Nor spoke carelessly.

Once you trusted her
She took a liking to you
A fondness even
Could relax in your presence
Seemingly let down her guard.

I guess she loved you.
Each time I saw you with her
Her hand leading you
How she softly spoke to you
Though at times she looked away.

Now that she is gone
Often you pause to glimpse her
As if in a dream.

Easy Conquest

She let you fool her
And fell for each lie you told
Eagerly even.

With her hands in yours
She dreamt of eternal love
Love you would give her.

Pleasure does not last
Her cute face quickly bored you
Her words sounded dull
Though she wept pleaded and begged
You were happy to leave her.

One sees her at times
Never a tear nor a sigh
Nor a thought for you.

A Pearl Thrown Away

I recall her words
One thing was completely clear:
She did prefer you.

And yet you left her
Went to look for a new fling
It lasted briefly.

When it unraveled
You acted so nonchalant
As if to fool me.

Danger

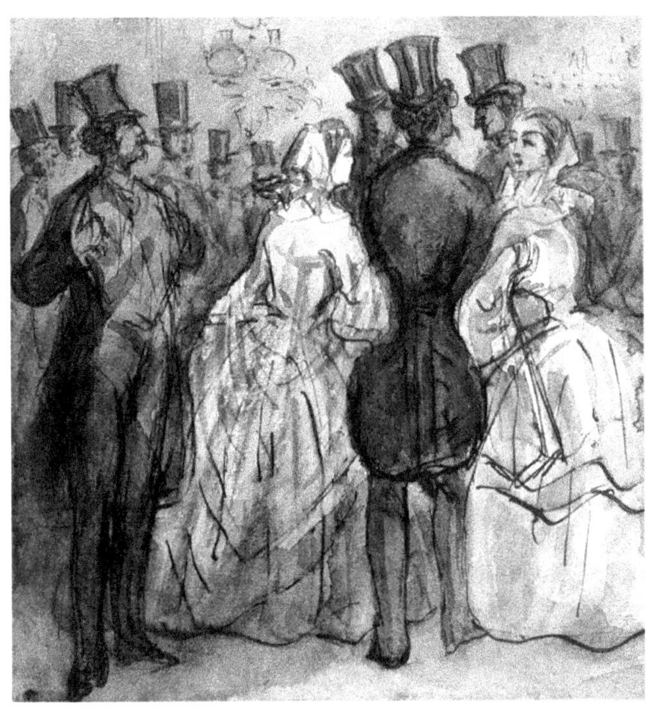

Clandestine Meeting

For her honored guest
She will gladly serve Champagne
Bubbles to the brim.

Tender Dover sole
Quickly delicately cooked
Sprinkled with sea salt,

There is a short pause
A need to add gentle words
As he relaxes,

White chocolate mousse
Smooth sugary satisfying
Lingering flavor.

She is fond of him
Closely watches over him
Takes his hand in hers
Lavishes kindness on him
Probes and exploits weaknesses.

Things Seen and Unseen

She loves to watch you
Keep her gaze focused on you
Observe perceive probe.

Though you may look back
You cannot know her secrets
But she has learned yours.

Foiled Security Measures

Her soft gloves touch him
Gently keeping him in place
Massage and bind him
Cover and caress his eyes
Then soundlessly gather loot.

When ready to leave
She shows him her fondness and
Kisses him goodnight.

This Lady Hates the Sight of Blood

With both her gloved hands
And his well-knotted neckties
She holds him secure
He really should relax now,
Now that he is less wealthy.

She makes not a sound
Even kisses both his cheeks
As she gets away.

Unsuccessful Money Saving

Those museum guards
Young men at their part-time jobs
Working the night shift
Noticed a gorgeous lady
Oh, yes, they saw her coming.

The following day
They awakened well-rested
Bound with their neckties
Did not seem bothered at all
But gave very few details.

Lady in a Scandal

Aware of the jokes
At times a bit ill at ease
Even so, quite proud.

Related Events

Needles inserted
Toxins quickly circulate
The inmate's heart stops.

New reports go out
After years of discussion
The matter is closed.

The real culprit laughs
His frame-up job fooled the court
He lives off his crime.

Testimony Prepared

His blood stops flowing
Leaves a large stain on the floor
The gun barrel cools
Her thoughts turn to the future
She will show her scars in court.

Tropical Calm

Her ice cream drips down
On her magenta swimsuit
Sea breezes pick up
Noontime sunlight strikes her eyes
Another lady watches.

She starts to doze off
On this languid afternoon
And slowly grows cold.

In a Luxury Hotel Suite

Her work completed
She sees his blood has congealed
His body grows cold.

Her dress still spotless
She has emerged unblemished
Left no evidence
All she holds dear she retains
Also her virginity.

Calm, sober, content
She softly closes the door
No one sees her leave,
Though satisfied, she shudders,
She remembers her sister.

The Sea

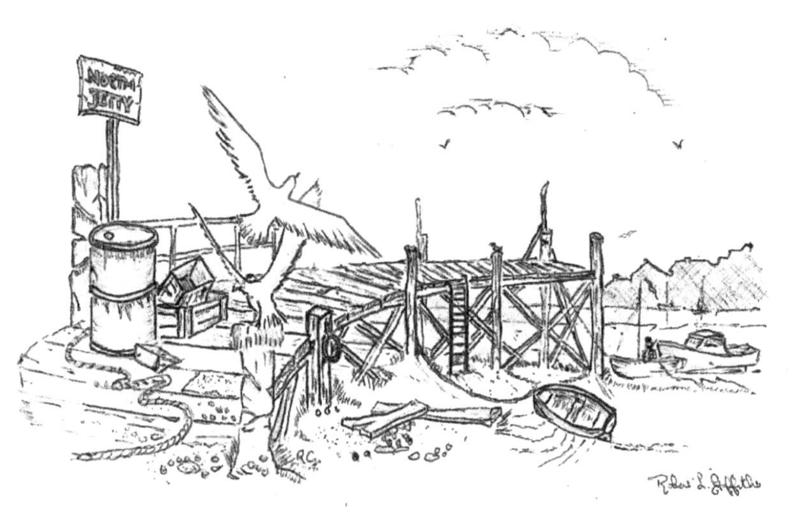

Unstable Conditions

As seagulls glide past
Winds kick up to push the waves
White foam masses crash
Pound the shore, knock down swimmers
Draw back, rush forward again,

Rushing from the sea
Winds accelerate, waves rise
Water strikes the sand
Yet gliding, never straining,
Seagulls venture forth to hunt.

Favorable Conditions

Ripples drift landward
Under seagulls' sunlit wings
Cargo ships reach port.

Precarious Moments

Standing in the sea
Waves and foam swirl around her
She stares to the west,
His ship on the horizon
Should elude the coming storm.

Alert Issued

Swirling on the map
The hurricane moves northward
Approaches the coast.

In its presumed path
An uncanny silence reigns
Until gusts pick up.

Albatross Spotted

Far from land and sea
Among clouds and swirling winds
In effortless flight.

There Is Still Time

Exhausted lifeguards
Frustrated in their efforts
Return to the beach.

After the first search
The helicopter returns
Winds intensify.

A new search must start
In spite of the bad weather
Substitutes arrive
The team is ready once more
A rescue is possible.

Mermaids

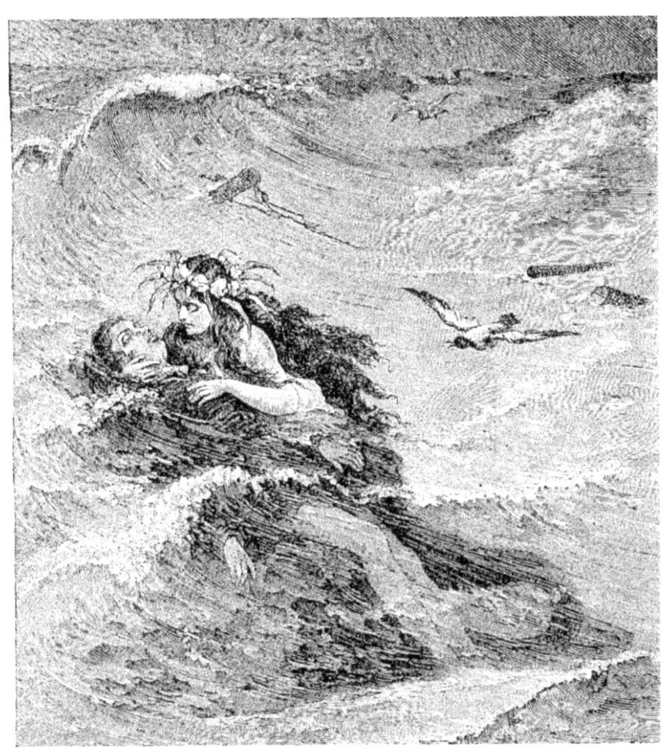

A Mermaid Amuses Herself

He thought he grasped her
Yet soon she swam to the depths
Waves pushed him ashore.

She Is Content to Flirt

Perched on a steep rock
Looking onto the calm sea
Her songs echoing
All warmed by the southern sun
Captains prefer to slow down.

A Mishap Was Triggered

There was no danger
All arrived safely on shore
The yacht was insured
Yet this scene does make her laugh:
Soaked dresses and tuxedos.

A Mermaid Chides a Rival

A swimsuit princess
Strolls in calm shallow water,
A fin-induced splash
Drenches her newly-coiffed hair
Makes her cosmetics drip down.

Further Amusement

From the placid depths
She accelerates upward
Shoots through the calm air
Flips above a pleasure boat
Leaves two fishermen baffled.

Not Passing Unseen

She surveys a beach
Observes a dream-filled young man
Staring at the sky
Hearing the loud cries of gulls
Venturing out to the sea

The waves push him back
Today she will not greet him
Allows him to roam.

She Also Dreams of You

Though far out to sea
Where she frolics amid waves
Her thoughts turn to you.

You did not notice
As you wandered on the beach
Slowly, aimlessly,
At times finding a seashell
How she kept you in her sight.

Throughout the long day
You could not escape her view
Under bright sunlight
Not one thing passed unremarked
She now knows you very well.

Tomorrow at dawn
When once again you set forth
She may beckon you.

A Close Call

Not far from the shore
She locks me in her embrace
Pulls me farther out.

"Let me possess you
Bring you deep into my realm
You will not escape
Know that both my hands grasp you
You need not think of leaving.

You cannot see land
But do look into my eyes
Let me enchant you
My fin brush against your legs
I will never leave your thoughts."

She pulls me farther
Waits for currents to change
Then releases me.

An Old Man on the Beach

She still sings to him
Never fails to notice him
He always listens
This mermaid fondly recalls
A helpless boy she once saved.

A Mermaid on the Loose

On a placid sea
With no waves or clouds in sight
She spots a sailboat.

Eager for some fun
With a quick dexterous push
She tips that sailboat.

A man falls headlong
Face-first into saltwater
She just has to laugh.

He must thrash about
Experience full panic
Until she holds him.

After he calms down
She makes sure he looks into
Both her sea-green eyes.

She will not let go
Kisses and overwhelms him
Lets him feel her strength
Her firm affectionate squeeze
Her fin caresses his feet.

Most flabbergasted
He tries to hold on to her
She slithers away.

Into deep waters
She plunges most rapidly
He cannot see her.

Wearily he sighs
Imagines it was a dream
Then she shoots upward.

Ten feet she rises
Seems to float above the sea
To view him again.

As she does a flip
And sees how happy he is
She waves him farewell.

Complete Change

Without knowing it
He has found his Calypso
Loving, enticing,
Now slides into her arms
Unaware of what she thinks.

A Mermaid's Conquest

She keeps him afloat
Amid swells and cresting waves
Lightning bolts above
Long after the storm has passed
She will keep holding him safe.

A Mermaid Greets a Sailor

Perched upon a cliff
She sees a ship approaching
The tide has gone out.

In foggy twilight
No captain could see the sandbars
The ship stays in place.

No winds or currents
Cause air or water to move
Sea and fog are still.

Calm, pensive, relaxed,
She recalls far-off shipwrecks
A song stirs in her.

A sailor stands watch
Slowly her song becomes clear
Her soft, mournful song.

She sings of widows
Sons and daughters left behind
Ships yet to return.

His eyes see nothing
The plaintive song pleases him
A sweet melody
Lovingly, thoughtfully sung
Peaceful, yet ardent, forceful.

Strange, archaic words
Recount tales of distant seas
Men and ships gone forth.

Very few returned
Many simply disappeared
He listens and sighs
The mermaid's song continues
He cannot help but hear it.

Slowly the fog lifts
Currents nudge the ship forward
Fresh winds fill the sails.

As sunlight strikes him
The mermaid's melody fades
He feels the ship sway
Looks to the cliff's jagged edge
She bids him a fond good-bye.

Romance

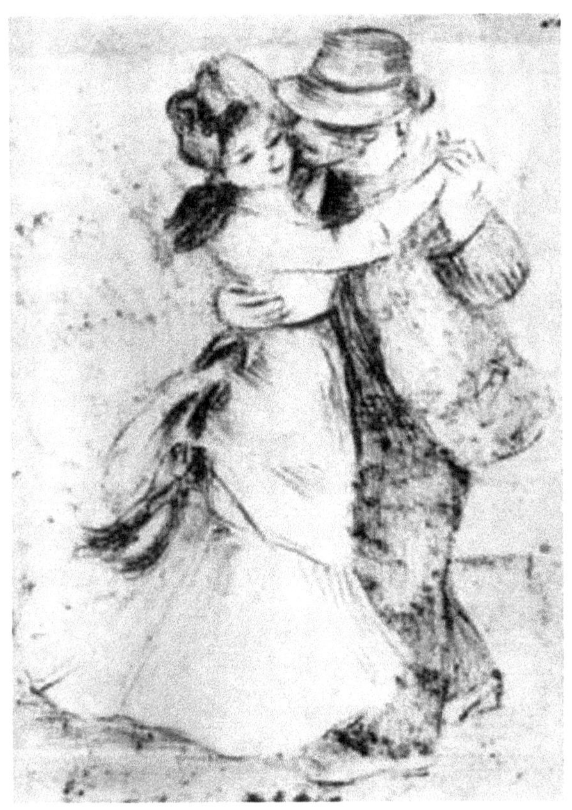

Successful Start

A bright orange dress
Stark contrast to her black hair
Coaxes approval,
A young gentleman greets her
Timidly takes her gloved hand.

A Promise She Will Keep

Dessert now finished
Their pleasant chat must conclude
He leans close to her,
She calmly raises her hand
Smiles and touches his cheek.

Complete Change

Without knowing it
He has found his one true love
Gentle, enticing,
Now slides into her arms
Unaware of what she thinks.

An Affectionate Wife

Dark blue satin gloves
Placed lovingly on his cheeks
She caresses him
Begs him to declare his love
Hears his answer, kisses him.

Happiness Will Continue

Her new white swimsuit
Contrasting with her black hair
Soaked after a swim
She embraces her husband
Ah, she knows he adores her.

Saturday Afternoon

She sits in the shade
Feels soft breezes from the sea,
Splashing among waves
Her husband and children play
Her watchful eyes adore them.

A Pleasant Habit

Each day at this time
The lady holds her husband
Safely in her arms
Confides to him how she is
Pleased to love this gentleman.

As Has Happened Before

She knows when to speak
Offers reassuring words
Turns his thoughts to her
Gently takes his hand in hers
Can see her charms persuade him.

Elegant Enticement

Happy to see him
She beckons softly persuades
Reassures coaxes
Takes in her faithful embrace
This man she keeps enchanted.

Interlude

She must interrupt
He needs no television
Her hands touch his cheeks.

She stands before him
He can see only her face
Her inviting grin
Oh, he easily succumbs
Her charms proved too much for him.

The Evening Has Begun

Let her beckon you
Stare into her dream-filled eyes
Take her by the hand,

She might stay with you
Choose to make you fortunate
Once she gains your trust.

Culinary

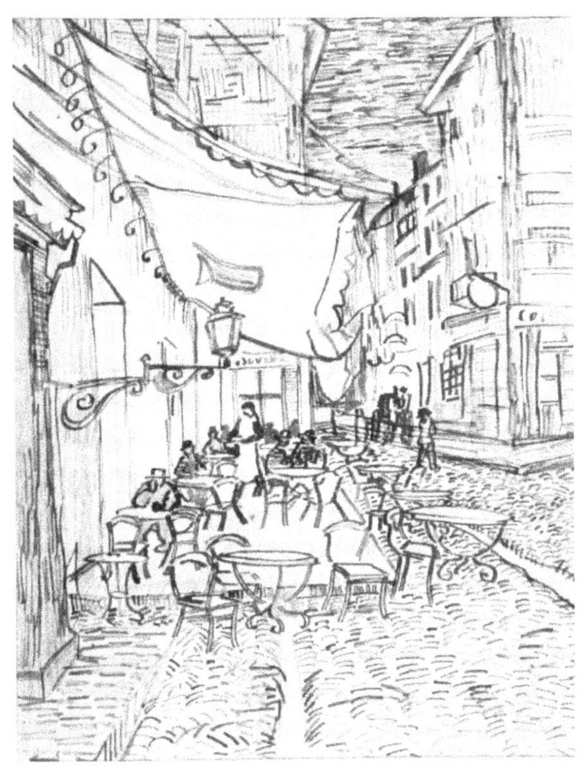

Thanksgiving Dinner

The oaken doors closed
Heavy rain strikes the windows,
We bid you welcome.

This November feast
Replete, even excessive,
Is offered to you.

A steam-filled oven
Slowly baked the plump turkey
Please slice moist, soft meat.

Boiled cranberries
Blended with dark brown sugar
Have cooled, are now served.

Peeled oversize yams
Mashed with thick maple syrup
Form mounds on your plate.

Bread, liver, cognac
Smoothly blended for stuffing
Mixed with apple bits.

Dark brown gravy drips
Onto slices of white meat
Soaks still hot stuffing.

Peas, onions, carrots
Add their part to the medley
Present bright colors.

For dessert, fruit pies,
Tart cherry, sugared apple
Whipped cream topped pumpkin.

Haiku Poems Inspired by Champagne

Yes, Dom Pérignon,
A chaste monk in his cellar,
Made his wine sparkle.

On the hard chalk hills
Stoic Champenois produce
Their effervescence.

Stroll in a vineyard
Here near Reims you just might find
A poilu's remains.

A scarred cathedral
Offers us testimony
Of war and healing.

Cathedral in Reims,
Gothic art amid vineyards,
Faith took deep roots here.

Watch the bubbles rise
Share the night with your good friends
Enjoying God's gifts.

Another Morsel

Thinly sliced salmon
Tender flesh, white streaks of fat
Soft, melting texture.

Dawn in a Pullman Car

Snow drifts line the route
First class passengers look out
Sip dark expresso.

Pinot Grigio

Clear chilled dry white wine
Smoothly blends with poached salmon
Swirls with seasonings.

Shrimp Tempura

Crispy white coating
Keeps a piece of shrimp juicy
Crunch it then slurp it.

Soft Shell Crab

Yielding to your knife
Yet crisp, hot, lightly seasoned
Filled with tender flesh.

Barbecue

Turning on a spit
The pig roasts amid gray smoke
Fat drips on the flames.

Charcoal still gives heat
The long cooking has finished
Knives are taken out.

The table is set
Smooth tender slices are cut
Steam rises from them.

Large plates are covered
Pork, beans with brown sugar, bread,
Collard greens, coleslaw.

Fill up beer glasses
Sauce oozes onto cutlets
Aromas beckon.

Manet's Bar

Staring at the crowd
Well-dressed, prim, perfectly groomed,
A barmaid at work.

Bottles all around
Ale, champagne, spirits, others,
Soon to be opened.

No orders right now
Her thoughts have drifted elsewhere
Reverie ensues.

A trace of sorrow
All her expression reflects
Until patrons come.

Rosé

Light pink in color
Rosé wine, pale, delicate,
Blends into dinner.

Its dry, subtle taste
Goes with appetizers, then
Grilled fish and scallops.

Rosé can assuage
Tabasco and hot peppers
While gently flowing.

After deferring
To others, rosé pleases
Palate and spirit

Giving its flavor
Product of intense labor
Even so, refined.

Rosé harkens to
Memories of summer sun,
It gave us this wine.

Friday Fish Dinner

Thin flounder filets
Fry, sizzle in coated pans
Come out slightly charred.

Alongside green peas
White rice, tomato slices
The main course is served.

Drops of Cajun sauce
Little dots among the colors
Scattered on your plate.

No sharp knife needed
Flat fishes, soft, mild, seasoned
Easily enjoyed.

Chilled white Sancerre wine
Follows smooth fish, side dishes
Adds a light sweetness.

Your Table Awaits

Dinner in Paris is always a pleasure,
There will be memories to treasure.
The waiters are simply the best
With wit and grace, they pass each test.
They have brilliantly mastered their art
And, yes, know the menu by heart.
Though in the bistro there is much noise
The staff keeps its coolness and poise.
Their discipline is clear to see
When one says "Je vous en prie."
And once they come to know you well
Each has many stories to tell.
You behold a pleasant smile
Learning French was all worthwhile.
If, however, you failed the French language test
Your profound apologies should be expressed.
I guess you chose to beware
Of the language of Molière.
Please, though, never address a waiter as "Garçon!"
To that I must interject "Mais, non!"
Well, you know not as much as you should
But fret not, since the food they serve is good.
You have the right to order draft beer
And speak the language of Shakespeare.

Widows

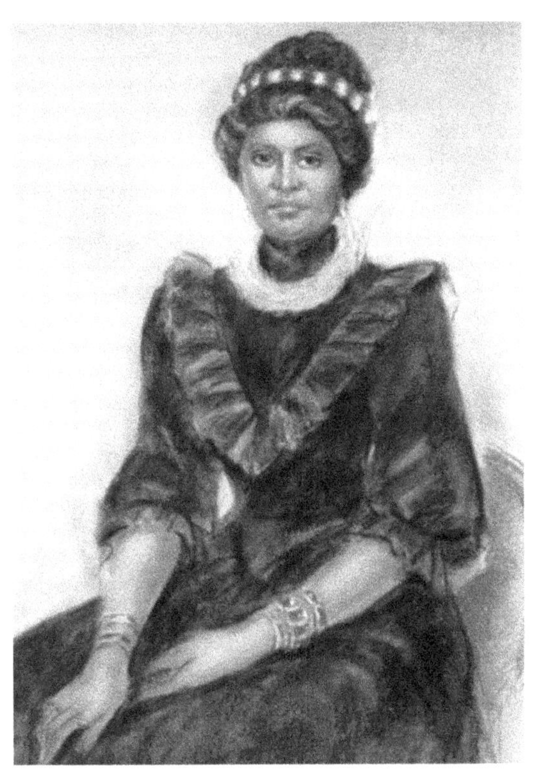

At Home

She presses his shirts
Keeps his woolen suits spotless
Arranges his ties
Thinks back to nights on the town
Rehearses dance steps alone.

At Her Desk

She sees his picture
Still a young man, no gray hair
His sly witty grin
Always won someone over
Other girls had much to say.

In the Park

Dreamily strolling
Leaning on her wooden cane
She sees a couple
Fondly recalls the old days
A guy makes his girlfriend blush.

In a Coffee House

She is not alone
Views passersby on the square
Sips steaming coffee
Recalls flirting with waiters
And re-reads her husband's books.

Her Afternoon

Her son at her side
Her cane not touching the ground
She walks gracefully
Extends greetings to others,
Kind words to all who respond.

On Vacation

She dresses for him
Black stockings, shoes, green silk dress
Matching velvet gloves
The waiters make way for her
They set a table for two.

In Late Autumn

Winds push leaves away
From quiet sidewalks and streets
With hair veiled, she stands
As the sun slips behind clouds
And breezes caress her face.

Her Morning

She ties his bowtie
The same feel on her fingers
Smooth, black, unblemished
She ties it for the last time
On her grandson's wedding day.

The Muse

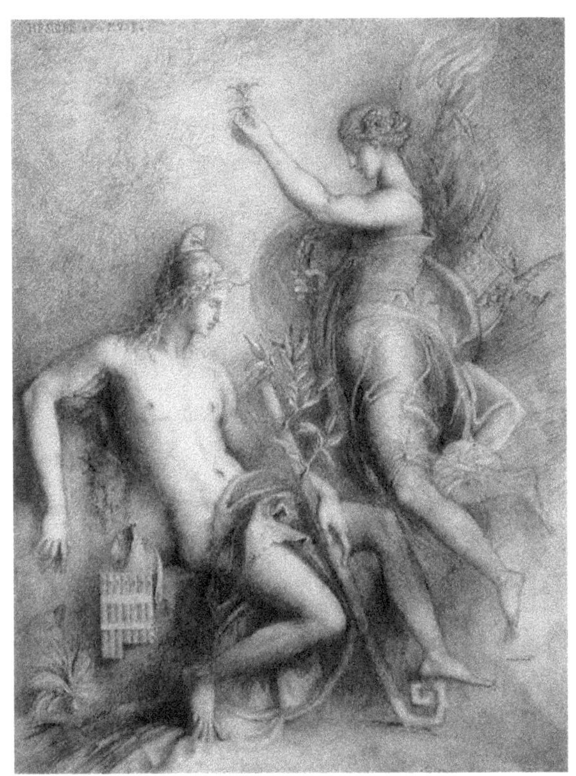

The Muse Observes a Widow

What is left to her,
Now that her poet has gone?
Where can her thoughts turn?

What a boy he was
Quick to laughter quick to tears
Eager for her love
Yet soon rushing off again
Chasing some sweet obscure song.

Quite inattentive
He seldom left his dream world
Wandered, drifted, wept,
He never noticed danger
Illness struck and he succumbed.

Her thoughts turn to dreams
Melodies rise in her soul
Songs borne by the wind.

A Stroll through Paris

A pleasant visit
Where she feels so much at home,
The Muse in Paris,
Here so many words came forth
She knows of course more will come.

In street side cafés
The old tradition lives on:
Young poets struggle.

Weary lovelorn men
Stare at the ceiling, ignore
Saddened girls who sigh
Each stays in his solitude
Or will give her heart again.

Few will hear her speak,
They must express her sorrow
Give wings to her thoughts.

Many fail badly
Put forth silly senseless words
Hail their own success
The Muse finds them most absurd
She has seen this sort before.

Few can hear her voice
They can think of nothing else
Give themselves to dreams.

Beside empty cups
Poetasters strive to write
Put words to paper
She sees how the waiters laugh
The words sound quite contorted.

Yet she has found one:
A young man lost to the world
Bound to her spirit.

The Muse comes to him
She whispers, insists, persuades
He hears her and writes.

The Muse Lies in Wait

She sees him wander
Blankly stare at the ocean
Unaware of her.

She observes him well
Ponders the thoughts in his mind
None of which he hides
Memories of lonely times
Plainly evident sorrow.

No words come to him
Only random images
Waves touching the shore
Seagulls beneath cloud-cloaked skies
Scattered raindrops fall on rocks.

She waits a bit more
As only she understands
A spark will suffice.

Explanation

"It was quite easy."
The Muse confided to me
"To lead you around.

Your eyes were open
Even so, rather vacant,
Confused, hesitant.

I dawdled with you
Let seasons and years pass by
I always have time.

When the moment came
The words flowed in a torrent
Swept you forcefully.

You were not clever.
I fully inveigled you
Then you went along.

You, faithful poet,
Simple, trusting, credulous,
The Muse's servant.

Your hand stays in mine.
I have not finished with you,
You will follow me.

New paths await you,
Obstacles, dangers, treasures,
Listen to my words."

The Muse and Her Poet

Standing behind him
Each hand sheathed in pink velvet
She covers his eyes
Thanks him for his devotion
Whispers playful promises

Wandering

During barren years
I wandered, avoided harbors
Let the winds guide me

The Muse surveyed me
Allowed me to drift about
Not one word came forth

No maps, no compass
My eyes let caprice guide me
To erratic ways

On dark forest paths
Beneath green, snow-covered pines
Gray, slow-moving clouds

On damp brown boardwalks
Near cresting, white-foamed masses
Dull, rain-soaked beach sands

In city alleys
Amidst fine-chiseled façades
Ivy-leaf shaped stone

Calm, lonely viewing
Seeing what many ignore
Meandering far

The Muse surprised me
Wove my thoughts into poems
Shook my weak spirit

My eyes focus outward
I hope to glimpse her again
Now she eludes me

Poets' Struggle

Poets can be fools
Wandering about with words,
Counting syllables.

Their dull vacant eyes
Notice little of the world
Or their place in it.

They seldom converse
Just add their misplaced remarks
People ignore them.

Eyes to the heavens,
Ears waiting to hear the Muse,
They drift in a daze.

God in His Wisdom
Puts these strangers in our midst
His wayward spokesmen.

Unworthy

The Muse holds her court
Poetry scholars arrive
Present petitions.

Deep analyses
Surely delved in mysteries
Led to treatises.

Their hard years of work
Secluded in libraries
Must merit rewards.

A dismissive wave
All the Muse deigns to give them
She says not a word.

Startled, embarrassed
The deflated scholars leave
For oblivion.

Errors

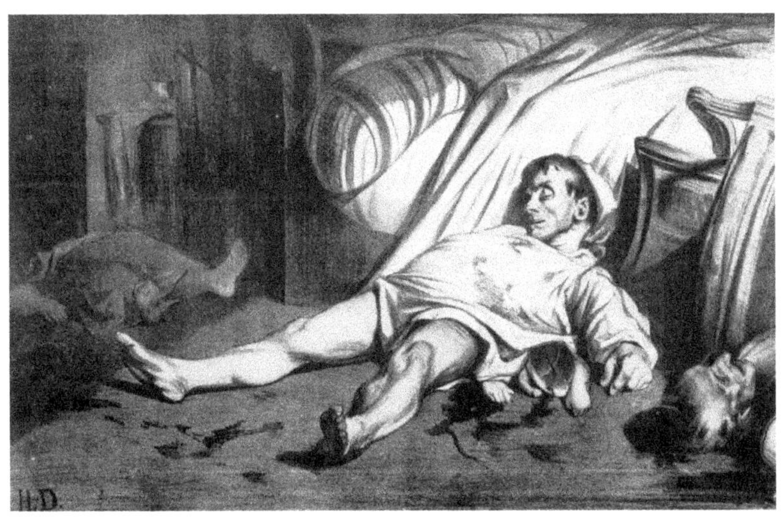

Enforcing the Law

A poetry bust:
The police in Montmartre
Raided a reading.

Behind Sacré Coeur
The criminals read their works
Shocking listeners.

Gosh-awful poems
Pompous, swollen, pretentious
They read out their *STUPIDITÉS*

The well-armed gendarmes
Subdued literary crooks
Hauled them off to jail.

To prevent more crimes
The judge decided to use
Summary justice:

Felony offense
First degree turgidity
No chance of parole.

Justice is dispensed
Literary quality
Survives in Paris.

My Generation's Shortcomings

Yes, Mrs. Parker,
We need your sharp-edged humor.
Boredom reigns these days.

Sad, dreary moaning
Can pass for some repartee
Then f-bombs go off.

A few poisoned darts
Soaked in playful levity
Need to hit their mark,

Or poetic gusts
Must expel tepid air
Give breath to laughter.

Light-hearted banter
Should fill our festive hours,
Words that could please you.

The Ghost of Poems Past

Out of murky swamps
Of fetid turgidity
He rises again.

From his gaping mouth
Words of folly issue forth
Thanks to bad poets.

To suburban homes
The dull, awkward specter roams
Into rooms with tomes.

Behind bolted doors
Inept writers find refuge
Deem themselves secure.

Did they write badly?
Well, they like each other's works -
Now the ghost walks in.

Poetasters gasp
Once again, they hear their words,
And this time, they cringe.

Verbiage assaults,
Deeply stabs its creators
Their minds come unhinged.

Shame, guilt, fear, disgust,
Rise in poetasters' souls
Their own words haunt them.

The ghost drones all night
His audience moans in pain
Begs for forgiveness.

He will not stand mute.
He must let loose all the words.
Yes, he quotes them all.

A merciful dawn
Makes the fearsome ghost depart
Blessed silence reigns.

Less Is Indeed Less

Mute Haiku poets
Join up with minimalists
To give these results:

Blank silence blank blank
Silence can be heard here blank
Blank blank silence blank.

Alternative Methods

When minds grow twisted
They seek out hovering signs
Adhere to bent rules.

Scornful of strict lines
They fuse words, light, random thoughts
Plunge through vast oceans

Heeding no compass
Swimming past sharks' snapping jaws
To settle in reefs.

Oxygen amassed
Orange flames are ignited
Strive to the surface.

Stolid earthen minds
Perceive unexplained jetsam
Rising in the air.

Hot cinders ascend
Far from their deep catalysts
Unto greater heights.

Yet in pleasant depths
Contorted minds seek new forms
Would grasp potent means.

Immobile

Wanton earthbound eyes
Probe into farther reaches
Bid visions to come.

Dynamite in place
Bright colorful explosions
Spectacles commence.

Yellow red orange
Flames dart across the heavens
Blue and green blend in.

Varied colors blend
But all blazes to purple
Which forms subtle shadows.

Eyelids strain wider
Minds seek to absorb fine tones
Flesh remains in place.

Pink white smoke rises
Then succumbs to gentle rain
Their elements clash.

A damp mist expands
Acidic compounds sting eyes
Tears form, minds fade out.

Not Clearly Perceived

Poets in a fog
Try to write psychedelic
Thrash their minds about.

They seek to achieve
Self-induced trips off to bliss
And they do succeed.

As for their poems,
Well, gosh, gee, these things happen
They gave off drivel.

Bad Haiku on Parade

The sun is setting
I feel so melancholy
The day is now done.

I regret this bilge
That I give to the critics
May they gag on it.

Bad Haiku alert
With turgidity warning
Remains in effect.

We hear sirens blare
The sound of "Turgid! Turgid!"
Echoes in the night.

This bad poetry
Will drive readers to despair
And rivers of tears.

Poetic sorrow
Caused by some bad metaphors
Can fill an ocean.

Like a simile
Poems can fall like drunkards
Into a cesspool.

Bad grammar poems
Don't got no, like, precision
To give no meaning.

Some old-time slang words
Let us get the drift, dig it,
Of a poem's flow.

Death by poetry
Your works may inflict this fate
Do not take the chance.

Absinthe

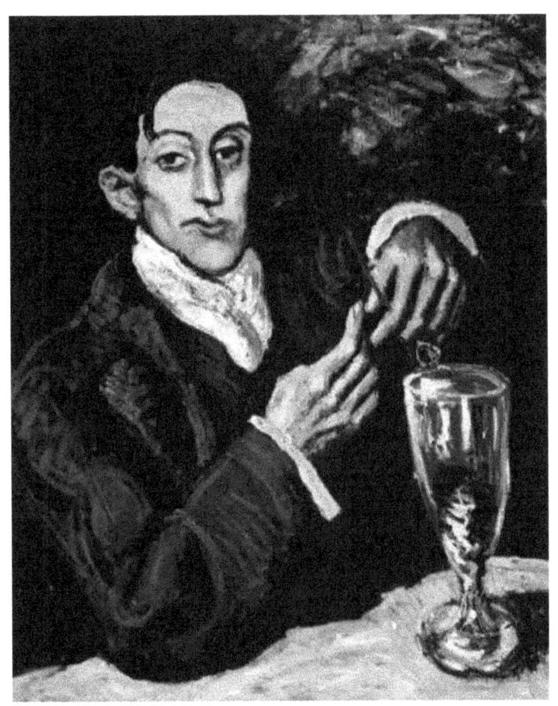

Introduction

She leisurely lurks
Often spots creative minds
Eager for her help
She is faithful in her deal
Your Muse, demon and mistress.

She sharpens your thoughts
Overloads your fragile flesh
And will discard you.

Separation

Your green fairy laughs
A wrecked spirit lies on the floor
Dazed eyes stare downward.

Around a spilled glass
Pens and papers lie scattered
Clocks' hands move no more
Your works remain half-written
That green fairy laughs, goes off.

Politics

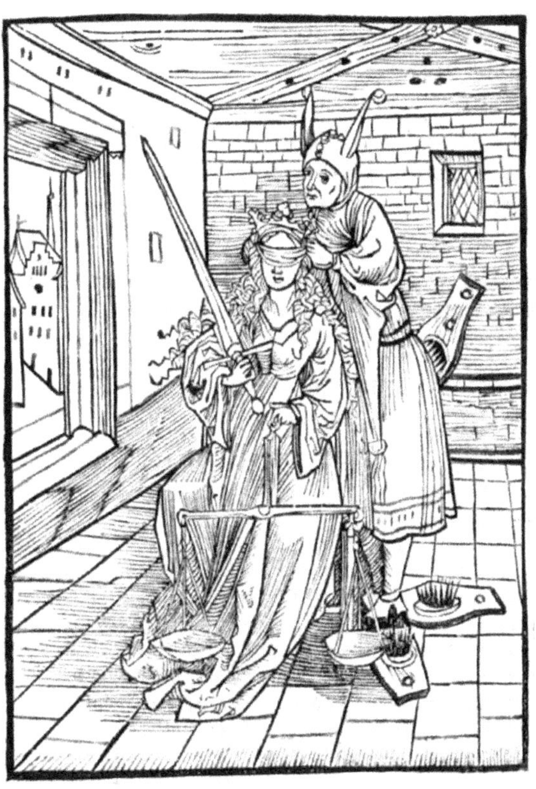

A Common Event in America

Alone in his call
The inmate sees minutes pass
Midnight approaches.

Guilty verdict stands
No stay of execution
All appeals used up.

Debates continue
Was the trial really fair?
His time ticks away.

Tied to a gurney
Prepped as if for surgery
He will feel no pain.

It all ends quickly
Monitors show a flat line
No heartbeat, no breath.

Attorneys argue
Perhaps with better counsel
He could have been saved.

His corpse is wheeled out
Embalmed, placed in a coffin
A grave was reserved.

Bloggers make comments
Find the sentence harsh but fair
Give their approval.

Protesters go home
They had hoped for clemency
Perhaps a delay.

The governor sleeps
He turned in early tonight
Calm, unaffected.

Another inmate
Tracks the course of his appeals
The judge will soon rule.

Government Assistance Denied

You followed the rules
Showed us how you need help
Filled out all the forms.

You have no money
You will soon be evicted
You worked all your life.

Well, we have rules here
Laws followed to the letter
No exceptions made.

We reviewed your case
But found a glitch in the law,
It is not your fault.

We cannot help you
Yes, we should help the needy
Let them keep their homes.

You must lose your home
Take your belongings with you
At winter's onset.

PR Damage Control

No alarm sounded
Toxic fumes filled the building
Workers gasped for breath
When reports reached management
Profound regrets were expressed.

Casualties Are Expected

We see war via Internet and television
Hear the generals explain each decision.
They choose their words with consideration
Think of the aspects of each operation.
Plans are made for each contingency
A response for any emergency.
Officers know that lives are at stake
Efforts are made to avoid a mistake.

Of course a heavy price must be paid
Regardless of how decisions are made:
As soon as we happen to see
A soldier suffering from PTSD
We realize that the reports are very real
Comprehend how the wounds will never heal.
No doctor knows what to say
The condition worsens day by day,
Once lucid eyes show a vacant stare
The hospital staff ponders medical care,
The little relief they can possibly give
Though this soldier has many years to live.

Read by Later Generations

A wartime letter
Sent from close to the front lines
Just a few kind words
Written in love and in haste
The bloodstains can still be seen.

Seeking Meaning

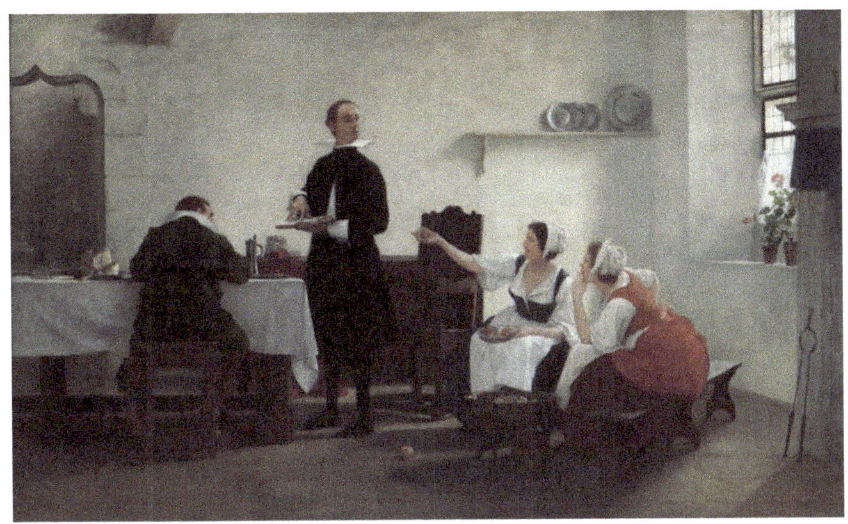

Overheard at an Exhibition

Though the works are as lovely as can be
Someone will inevitably disagree.

"With its brushstrokes of ochre
This painting is most mediocre."

"For such an image I do not care
I find it arid, abstract and bare."

"I perceive a void in this visual expression
It allows no aesthetic concession."

"For his ineptitude there exists no cure
This painter will remain obscure."

For such harshness we can find no prevention
We must dread each critic's condescension.

Museum Mishap

We beheld works of the highest art
But then phones were no longer smart.
Each visitor assumed a statuesque form
In the midst of this sudden IT storm,
Not one could utter so much as a sound
Whilst wisdom was not to be found.
No on-line interpretations were consulted
A full lack of understanding then resulted.
The silence of the electronic waves
Could be compared to that of graves.
In the rooms featuring Turner and Constable
The confusion that reigned was most abominable.
Within the sight of Manet and Monet
All meaningful thoughts drifted far astray.
Can someone fathom the scene of Van Gogh's chair?
Or should we weep in sorrow and despair?
Sadly, people are fully in a daze
As if oblivious of Picasso's gaze.
No remedial measures have been planned
Such incapacity is common throughout the land.
Lest ye wail in anguished and pain-filled cries
Avail thyselves of the power of thine eyes.

Thoughts on "The Unconverted" by Francis Davis Millet

A parson whose life is abstemious and severe
Prompts the faithful to say "Good gosh! Oh dear!"
He never allows any single thing out of place
And always has a stern expression on his face.
His morals are as strict and rigid as a steeple.
He constantly mentions the sins of other people.
Never does this parson doubt his rectitude
Nor his theology in its exactitude.
Of his salvation he is thoroughly convinced
No hesitation is ever even slightly evinced.
He is ready for any disputation
To uphold his stellar reputation.
Temptation may have come his way
But never once was he led astray
Over his congregation he will hold sway.
We notice also with clarity
His appalling lack of charity
In his automatic statements of severity.
Take heed, therefore, lest you should bow
To one who is holier than thou.

Signed Up for the Wrong Course?

The professor speaks in a manner not at all clear
Which makes each student sigh and say "Oh drear!"
Wisdom and eloquence exist here not
Only the emission of air that is rather hot.
Worse yet in this atmosphere turgid and opaque
The professor's statements are esoteric and fake.
They could never serve as literary enhancement
But solely as blatant career advancement.
He simply repeats in replication
Words from his mentor's publication.
The nonsense of this academic scam
Will be regurgitated on the final exam.
Although it is thorough intellectual degradation
Luckily there is grade inflation.
For some in the class this course was required
But happily the semester will soon have expired,
And what sort of lessons can be learned
Once the professor's twaddle is purged and burned?
Students must obviously be more selective
When trying to fulfill an elective.

Tonight on TV

Murder mysteries
Really should not unnerve us
They're entertainment.

Small cups of hemlock
Discreetly served at dinner
Take care of some guests.

A car's tampered brakes
Give out somewhere near a cliff
Too late for repairs.

An agile burglar
Keeps things hushed throughout the house
Makes off with the loot.

There is a lady
Lying breathless on the floor
Her necktie too tight.

A respected man
Once rich, now his bloodline drained
Has his will revised.

The inspector comes
Points out the guilty party
Justice has prevailed.

Culprit arrested
It's late, we should go to bed.
Is the alarm on?

The Screenwriters Explain

Relax and don't be uptight
You will get a fright
This Halloween night.
Things will be bloody and nice
When the sharp knife gives a slice.
Such are the cinematic facts
Shown by a pyscho wielding an axe.
The audience is taken aback
With each and every whack
And when we need a new theme
A helpless victim will give a scream
Standing suddenly cheek by jowl
Next to a werewolf who gives a howl.
When of such things viewers do tire
Hear the laugh and see the teeth of a vampire.
Keep it coming, don't let up on the gore
A small body count means a big bore,
You know what they want to have in store.
It's always a box office dud
When you don't see enough blood.

Pick Up the Gauntlet

We never know how things really are
Whether viewed from near or far.
How will the fates change and churn
When lines of verse glow and burn?
How shall notions turn and twist
Whilst in a deep poetic mist?
Must readers meander in a fog
Fall off a bridge and into a bog?
Baffled onlookers must await a clue
The answer, they say, will come from you.

Art

Cover-*La Loge de l'opéra* ; Constantin Guys; 19th Century

Temptations- *Untitled;* Constantin Guys; 19th Century

Danger- *At the Theater (Au foyer du théatre; Ladies and Gentleman;* Constatin Guys, 1860-1892

The Sea- *Fishermen's Dock*; Robert Leslie Griffiths Sr, 1986

Mermaids- Illustration from p. 357 of Hans Andersen's Fairy Tales (1888).

Romance- *Country Dance*; Original Title: *Danse à la campagne;* Pierre-Auguste Renoir; 1883

Culinary- Preparatory study for the painting *Café Terrace at Night*; Vincent van Gogh; 1888

Widows- Nancy Wahinekapu Sumner Ellis, as a widow; Artist Unknown; 1889

The Muse- *Hesiod and the Muse*; Gustave Moreau; 1857

Errors- *Rue Transnoniain*; Honoré Daumier; 1834

Absinthe- *Portrait of Angel Fernández De Soto* or *The Absinthe Drinker*; Pablo Picasso, 1903

Politics- Illustration for Sebastian Brant's *Narrenschiff;* Artist Unknown, 1498

Seeking Meaning- *The Unconverted*; Francis Davis Millet; 19th Century

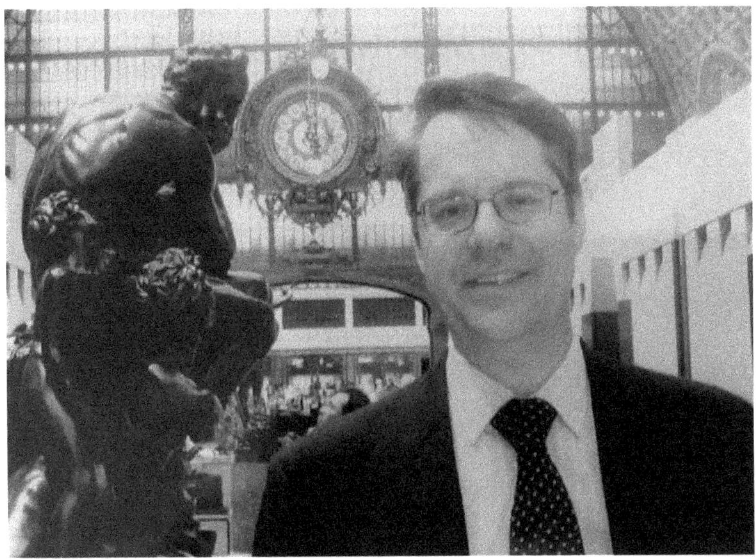

Mark Schardine is a New Jersey resident with a lifelong love of poetry, and the many pleasures it offers us. He believes that each of us is an heir to the remarkably beautiful tradition of poetry that previous generations have bequeathed to us, and seeks inspiration in works of the past. As part of his respect for the tradition, he greatly enjoys attending poetry events, listening to the works of others and at times presenting his own.

In 2015, he published his first French language book of poems, entitled *Au bord des rêves*, followed in 2019 by *Vers des horizons lointains*. Also, in 2019, his first English language poetry book appeared, entitled *Charm, Elegance, and Intrigue*. It was followed in 2020 by *As if in a Distant Dream*. This third book *Under Watchful Eyes* has more experimentation with different forms and subjects, varying from forms based on the Japanese styles of senryū, haiku, and tanka, as well as rhyming couplets, and with subjects as different as the beauty of nature, culinary pleasures, and the complexity of human relationships.

www.ingramcontent.com/pod-product-compliance
Lightning Source LLC
LaVergne TN
LVHW020510100826
845148LV00003B/748

* 9 7 8 1 7 3 7 4 7 5 8 4 2 *